The
Motivational Techniques
of
Urban Meyer

*A Leadership Case Study of the Ohio State Buckeyes
Football Head Coach*

Leadership Case Studies

Table of Contents

Introduction

Background Information about Urban Meyer

<u>Part 1: Keys to Performance</u>

- Leadership

- Accountability

- Performance

- Constant Learning

<u>Part 2: Resources</u>
- Quotes, Statements, and Ideas from Urban Meyer

- What People say about Urban Meyer

- Books recommended by Urban Meyer

- Key Takeaways

Additional Case Studies
About Leadership Case Studies

Introduction

In January 2015, Urban Meyer lead the Ohio State Buckeyes to the national championship. With the victory, Meyer has now coached teams to 3 national championships, adding to the 2 that he won when he was the head coach at University of Florida.

Along with Nick Saban, Meyer is considered to be the best coach in college football. With his ability to motivate his players and have them playing at a high level, Meyer has achieved success at every school he has coached at.

In his first head coaching job at Bowling Green, Meyer took a team that finished 2-9 the year before and got them to finish with a 8-3 record, the biggest turnaround in the nation that year. After 2 successful years at Bowling Green, Meyer left to coach the University of Utah. While at Utah, Meyer lead the team to an undefeated season and had his quarterback selected as the No.1 pick in the NFL draft.

After Utah, Meyer moved to Florida where he won two national championships and had his star quarterback win the Heisman trophy. Due to his intense competitive nature and work ethic, Meyer resigned in 2010 for health reasons and took a year off from coaching. Meyer took over the program at Ohio State at the start of 2012. The previous year, the Buckeyes had a 6-7 season. Since taking over the program, the team won their first 24 games with Meyer as the head coach, and became a championship winning team within 3 seasons.

The results are very clear. Meyer can coach. He can motivate young men to play hard and fast. He can create a culture that strives for excellence. And he can accomplish this immediately after taking over the leadership role.

In this brief leadership case study, we analyze and study the motivational techniques, strategies, and management ideas of

Urban Meyer. We find out how he is able to constantly create high performing organizations around the country, and how his teams are able to become championship winning teams.

The lessons from this leadership case study can be applied to anyone looking to compete at the highest level. Whether you are a coach, manager, or individual looking for personal improvement, the lessons of Urban Meyer can help you raise your performance. You do not have to be a fan of the Ohio State Buckeyes, or even to be a football fan to learn from this case study. Issues of motivation, effort, and accountability can be applied to any organization and personal goals.

This case study is broken up into 2 parts. In Part 1: Keys to Performance, we share the ideas and strategies that Urban Meyer brings to his programs. The keys are categorized into sections of leadership, accountability, performance, and learning.

In Part 2: Resources, we share direct quotes and statements made by Urban Meyer, as well as quotes made about him, that demonstrates his thoughts in the quickest and clearest way possible. These direct statements gives the reader a great profile of Urban Meyer and how he approaches his craft. We also include several books that Urban Meyer has publicly recommended.

After each section, we list a few review questions that you can ask yourself to help you apply the management tips of Urban Meyer directly to your own goals. In addition, at the end of the case study, we list a few of the key ideas and takeaways to help you quickly absorb the performance ideas from this leadership case study.

All sources listed in this, as well as links to the articles, videos and other documents are available at the website leadershipcasestudies.com.

Background Information about Urban Meyer

Date of Birth: July 10, 1964

College Education: Bachelor Degree in Psychology, University of Cincinnati, 1986. Master Degree in Sports Administration, Ohio State University, 1988.

Head Coaching Experience:

Bowling Green State University (2001 - 2002)
University of Utah (2003-2004)
University of Florida (2005-20100
Ohio State University (2012-Present)

National Championships

University of Florida (2006, 2008)

Ohio State University (2014)

Overall Record (Up to 2014 season)
141-26

Record in Bowl Games (Up to 2014 season)
9-2

Part 1: Keys to Performance

With 3 national championships under his belt, Urban Meyer is widely considered to be one of the best coaches in America. Opposing coaches, former and current players, and sports columnists point to several factors that contribute to the incredible success that he has achieved.

After collecting information through numerous articles about his success and listening to speeches given by Urban Meyer, we have compiled the best techniques and information that he has used to create teams and programs that compete at the highest level.

After each section we have listed several review questions that we feel would be beneficial to you and your organization. These questions highlight the issues that Meyer brings to his team, and may be helpful to you as you bring the lessons of Meyer to your own organization or personal journey.

Leadership

Clarity of Purpose

Urban Meyer is a big fan of the book Lone Survivor by Marcus Luttrell. The book details the work of Navy Seals who entered Afghanistan and was ambushed by the enemy. Meyer states that he finds great inspiration and motivation by the work of the military, and is constantly finding ways to motivate his players based on the teachings of the armed services.

One of the key messages that Meyer took from the book came on page 15. At the top of the page, Luttrell writes, "The clarity of purpose is inspirational." Meyer mentioned in a speech at a coaches clinic that a team lacking clarity of purpose is like forcing them to fight with one hand tied behind their back.

The clarity of purpose can be viewed as the mission statement for the organization. The goal and vision that Meyer has for his team is not based on an external result, such as winning a national championship. Rather his clarity of purpose is to get the his team to "perform at their maximum capacity."

The Ohio State football team is broken up in to 9 units based on positions. On offense, there are the quarterbacks, running backs, wide receivers, tight ends, and offensive line. On defense, there are the defensive linemen, linebackers, cornerbacks, and safeties.

Each unit has a coach who is dedicated solely to that unit. Meyer refers to the coach as the Unit Leader. The ideas that Meyer wants to instill into his team is based off of the methods that the US military, where each soldier's fights and trains with their unit.

Meyer wants each unit leader to be performing at a high level. He believes that if each unit is performing at maximum capacity, then there is no way that the team will lose. If only 6 out of 9 units are together and performing at their highest level, then the team will not be able to win tough games. But if 9 out of 9 units are at their maximum capacity, and trust each other, then the team will be formidable.

Three Traits in Developing Trust

In order to achieve results with your organization, the people in it must first trust you. Meyer firmly believes in having his players trust their coaches. The players need to trust their unit leader in order to play hard, to be committed, and to listen to the advice that the coaches give out.

In a speech to a coaches clinic held at Mississippi State, Meyer talked about the 3 ways that a leader can get his players to trust him. The ideas and strategies can work for any business or organization where a leader is looking to get people to buy into their vision.

1. You must be a person of character.

The people you are leading must believe that you have a strong personal character. They must have repeated experiences of watching you do the right thing. Meyer explains that when players repeatedly see their coaches being true to their word, then the players will begin to trust them. The unit leaders can demonstrate a strong personal character by treating all players with respect, doing what they say they will do, and being upfront with the players.

For example, if a coach tells a player that he will get the ball 20 times in a game, yet the player only touches the ball 3 times during the game, do you think that the player will trust the coach? What if a coach is recruiting a player, and tells the player he will start his Freshman year. However, the player doesn't see playing time during the season. Will the player play hard and believe in what the coach is asking? Then next time in practice where the coach tells the player to give a little more effort, will the player want to rise up to meet the challenge?

That is why Meyer believes that the player must believe that the coach is a person of character. The coaches and unit leaders can't make promises they can't keep. They can't say things to the players that they know aren't true. They need to do what they say they will do and not be hypocrites.

Regardless of the industry, if employees do not feel that their managers will behave and act in the right way, then that team is doomed from the start. If the employees feel that the manager is only looking out for his own interest, then that employee will not buy in to the mission and commit 100 percent. The fear and anxiety stemming from their questions about the character of their leader will keep them from fully trusting the organization and direction.

Only when the player, team member, or employee believes that the leader is a person of character will they fully buy in to the mission.

2. You must be competent.

The second task that you must do in order for people to trust you as a leader is to show that you are competent. Your players and staff must have the repeated experience of seeing you do your job well. They must see you prepared for your meetings with them, and see you do your own job with the highest effort and dedication.

Meyer used the example of current NFL head coach Bill O'brien as an example. O'brien is currently the head coach of the Houston Texans, but previously in his coaching career he was on the coaching staff of the New England Patriots. While with the Patriots,

O'brien was the Quarterbacks Coach and Offensive Coordinator to arguable one of the best quarterbacks in NFL history, Tom Brady.

Brady is known for his incredible work ethic and knowledge of the game. It was O'brien's responsibility to coach Brady and prep him for upcoming games. In a radio interview, O'brien stated that he needed to go the extra mile because he knew Tom Brady was going to be prepared. He knew that the best player in the NFL was going to be sitting in the film room, and if O'brien didn't have his facts together, or wasn't as committed to winning as Brady was, then there were going to be problems.

Meyer said that he was blown away when he heard that interview. Imagine coaching the best player in the world, he said. Imagine showing up to a meeting and not having your notes in order. Imagine that the player spent more time studying then the coach. Would that player trust that coach? Would they believe that the game plan was properly thought out and the best way to win?

Of course not. Meyer says that he instructed his position coaches to imagine that they were all coaching Tom Brady. Imagine that every player in their unit was the best in the nation and was on their way to the NFL. Imagine that the player prepared just as hard as the coach, and knew the playbook just as well as the coach. How hard would the coach have to work in order to be able to lead this player? The answer clearly is a lot, and this high level of effort then raises the performance across the entire organization.

Unfortunately, there are many times when the leader is not prepared. The personal trainer who shows up 15 minutes late for a 6:00 AM workout carrying a Starbucks. The manager who asks questions that were answered in the memo that was passed out earlier in the week. The salesman who clearly doesn't know the market and needs of the customer.

Whenever a person comes across a leader who is not prepared or competent, than the trust in the organization and leader immediately goes down. The lack of competency shows a lack of respect of the employees time, intelligence, and ambition.

If the leader can show that they are willing to work just as hard, if not harder than the employee, then trust can be created. The player or worker must believe that the leader knows what they are talking about, and took the time to fully think about their strategy.

3. You must connect with the person.

The third way to create trust with your subordinates is through connection. Your players and staff must know that you care about them. There must be repeated experiences of you showing them that you care about them.

Meyer makes it clear that by connection, he does not mean hanging out with them and drinking beers. It means doing things that can benefit them in the future. It means helping them write out a resume, or checking in on their parents when they visit, or taking the time to teach them time management skills.

By repeatedly showing your players that you care about them, Meyer believes that they will then be more willing to trust you. "You can move mountains with a football team if they know you care about them," Meyer says.

In his speech to the Ohio High School Coaches, Urban Meyer repeatedly said that the biggest issue facing a team when it's facing 3rd and 3 isn't a football issue, but a trust issue. The problem facing the team isn't what type of play to run, or what type of scheme to put in. THe problem is figuring out how much trust the players have the in coaching staff. Meyer said that if the team believes in the coaches, and the reason why they believe in the coaches is because they really believe that the coaches care about them, then picking up the 3 yards isn't a problem.

This means that regardless of the what type of play is called, the players will believe in the call. The players will believe that the coaches made the right decision because they are people of character. They players will believe that the coaches are competent and have put in the work and have prepared for this 3rd and 3 situation. And the players truly believe that the coaches care about the players and want them to succeed.

With the players believing in all three aspects, they fully trust whatever scheme or play that the coaches send out to the playing field. This allows them to play hard and fast, because any doubt in the coaching staff has been eliminated. They are able to pursue their objectives with relentless effort because they fully trust what their coaches are telling.

How Meyer Shows He Cares About his Players.

So how does Meyer show his players that he cares about them? One way is to spend the time with the players. As simple as it sounds, not many coaches take time to really touch base with their players. While filming the Ohio State Training Camp Special on ESPN, Meyer is seen talking to one of his players and telling him that they should call the player's Mom in the evening. Meyer wasn't telling the player to "call your Mom"; Meyer was telling the player to remind the coach as well because Meyer wanted to talk to the player's Mom as well.

This close contact with his players is something that Meyer has done throughout his career. At his first head coaching job at Bowling Green, Meyer took the time to help tutor one of his players into the late night.

From the Toledo Blade:

"Meyer, who earned a base annual salary of $125,000, spent a couple months as the team's strength coach, slept in the dorms during preseason camp, and interrupted position drills to demonstrate proper technique ... to the offensive line. He often spent nights tutoring players, one time spending 9 to 11 with Jovon Burkes reviewing the material for a statistics test the sophomore linebacker needed to pass the next day.

"And I was just a kid on the kickoff team," Burkes said."

Another way that Meyer demonstrates care for them is through a program called "Real-Life Wednesdays". The program provides the Ohio State football players with lectures and lessons to help them prepare for life after they leave the university. From teaching them about personal finance to writing a resume, Meyer has taken it upon himself to make sure that players know that he cares about them as human beings and not just as football players.

Before the start of the season, Meyer and his staff writes out a list of speakers who will come in every week and talk to the players. The speakers ranges from local business leaders, law enforcement officers, and communication professionals. These individuals talk to the players about their careers, how they got started, and provides them with practical tips on how to succeed in life after their football playing days are over.

Near the end of the season, the players dress up in a suit and tie and then go to a job fair that was Meyer puts on for them. There, the players are able to meet companies and government agencies and to explore possible careers after graduation.

Review Questions:

1. Do you have a "clarity of purpose"? If every member of your team was asked to write down the team's purpose, would everyone write the same thing?

2. How clear is your own individual purpose? Would the people reporting to you know what your purpose was? Would they know how you view your role as their leader, and what it is you want to accomplish for them? What about your friends and family? Are your goals so clear that everyone around you are fully aware of them and are helping you reach them?

3. How strong is your character when dealing with your team? Would every person in your team trust that you have their best interests at heart? How many people would say that you cared only about your own career and not theirs? Does all of your players know exactly where they stand, how you feel, and what you are doing? Or do they think you play games, don't tell them the truth, and that you have a hidden agenda?

4. How prepared are you when meeting with your players? Do you carefully plan each activity or project for them? How much time do you actually spend getting prepared and better at your own job? Do you ever just "wing it" in meetings with your subordinates?

5. Are you actually taking the steps to show your players, employees, or students that you truly care about their well-being? Are there specific things that you are incorporating into your program that shows you really do care about them? If a reporter asked them for a specific example where they felt like you demonstrated that you care about them, would they be able to provide examples?

Accountability

Direct Feedback

One of the most important aspects of Urban Meyer's program is to give his players feedback that clearly tells them how they are performing. He doesn't beat around the bush. He tells them exactly how they are doing, what they need to improve, and how they need to improve.

In a speech to high school coaches in Ohio, Meyer talked about how the state produced many great football coaches. One of the common traits all of these coaches had is the ability to have "honest, hard conversations".

These tough, difficult conversations are necessary to have with players in order to get them on the right page. Too often, these players listen to outside noise and do not have an idea about their playing abilities. Meyer says that an uncle might have told them they are good enough to get to the NFL, or maybe their parents are telling them that they should be starting.

Meyer believes that it is necessary for all players to know exactly where they stand. If they are not good enough to start, then they should clearly know that. If their effort is not high, then they should be called out on it immediately. If the player is slacking and isn't being a good teammate, then they should know that.

By not telling the player the honest truth, Meyer states that you are giving him "false confidence." In a radio interview that was transcribed by the website CoachingSearch.com, Meyer said "The worst thing that can ever happen is, when you say the word 'confidence' is false confidence. That'll destroy a player's career, because you're telling them this, and he's going to be this, and all of a sudden, he gets hit in the face and thinks, 'Wait a minute'."

Meyer states that the only way players and his team can improve is by receiving honest, direct feedback.

"The one thing I would say the mark of our program is absolute honesty. It's transparent," says Meyer. "Sometimes, people say 'Why do you say that about a player?' What do you want me to say? If he's not playing well, he's not playing very well. Our backup defensive linemen need to play better. It'd be terrible for me to go to the backup defensive linemen, pat them on the back and say, 'You had a great day today.' No, you didn't. It wasn't very good. We've got to be better tomorrow. In my opinion, that's why guys perform and improve."

Meyer states that this lack of honest feedback and evaluation is a major factor that causes teams, organizations, and individuals to fail. Meyer calls this symptom "a lack of truth".

One easy way to find out if there is a lack of truth in your organization is to have everyone conduct a self-evaluation. The coaches or management evaluates the individuals, and then compares their own evaluation with the self-evaluation of the player. If the two evaluations are far apart, then you have a problem.

Meyer stated that players who are not highly rated by the coaching staff consistently give themselves a higher evaluation, while those who are highly rated by the coaching staff give themselves lower grades.

When Meyer sees that an underperforming player gives himself a high evaluation, Meyer doesn't necessary place the blame on to the player. Rather, his first action is directed towards his coaching staff. He talks to the position coach who deals with the player the and basically asks him, "What the hell are you telling this kid?" If the coaching staff was properly teaching the player, and if there was constant feedback, then the player would have a strong understanding about their own performance.

As the CEO of the program, Meyer delegates the nuts and bolts of the coaching techniques to the unit leaders, while he manages and ensures that the unit leaders are performing up to his high standards. If a unit is not achieving excellence, then Meyer and his staff have difficult, uncomfortable conversations to discover the problems in the same way that the coaches talk to the players.

It is very hard to address any shortfalls or problems in a unit. Meyer says that "it takes time, effort, and guts to find out what the problem is." It's hard to do that because we naturally try to defend ourselves or find excuses for the low performance.

Meyer has a saying that he uses to explain excuses:

B.C.D. - Blame, Complain and Defend.

When you are faced with a problem, the worst thing that you can do is Blame others, Complain about the situation, or Defend yourself and say that it's not a problem. Meyer firmly believes that whenever you meet a problem, you face it head on and fix the problem.

Take Action to solve problems

In life and in football, Urban Meyer believes that there are only two types of people. Those that are part of the problem, and those that solves problems.

"On one side, you've got the real guys. You've got the solutions. You guys are going to bust your ass, do shit right all the time and find a way to win a game."

"On the other side, what do you got? You've got the pain in the ass. You've got the parent bitching about something. You've got this athlete who thinks he needs the ball more. You've got this stuff going on. You've got a guy drinking and putting drugs in his body. You've got this stuff going on. That falls in the pain in the ass category."

In addition, "when you're hit in the face - we all get hit in the face in work, family or social situations or team situations - there are only two choices," Meyer said in a speech after winning his 3rd national championship. "You can be part of the problem, or you can be part of the solution."

Meyer has no time to waste with players who fall in the "pain in the ass category". When he first started at Bowling Green, he would put his team through tough practices where several players simply quit the team. Meyer shed no tears for those who couldn't handle the pace.

"Good riddance," he said. "If they're not as committed as the guy next to them, we don't want them."

Review Questions:

1. Does everyone in your organization know exactly how they are performing? If everyone did a self-evaluation, and management did their own evaluation, how closely would the results line up?

2. What about your own evaluation? If your players or employers evaluated you, would their results line up with your own evaluation?

3. When was the last time you had a "hard, honest conversation" with someone in your program. Or maybe even with yourself? Are you avoiding addressing problems due to the potential difficulty in the conversation? Do you hope that these problems will just go away in the future?

4. How does your staff deal with problems? Are their immediate reaction to blame others, complain about the situation, or defend themselves? How are you planning on overcoming B.C.D. in order to address the issue? How do you react to problems as well? Are you just blaming your staff, complaining about the workforce, or defending yourself?

5. There are two types of people, according to Meyer. Problem solvers, and problem creators. How many are on your team? Does a problem creator immediately come into your mind? How can you change them into a problem solver? Think about yourself as well. Do you give up when faced with a problem? Or do you immediately

start thinking about solutions?

Performance

One of the key characteristics of Urban Meyer's football teams is their unrelenting effort. This attitude is not a coincidence. Meyer instills in his team an angry, determined, tough attitude by preaching those traits in everything that they do. He wants them to constantly strive to be the best, and is willing to use any motivation to create that sense of urgency.

"Did you push yourself to be great today? Did you do it?", Meyer asks his team after a training camp practice. "If you didn't, you lost a day, and we ain't got many days to lose."

A common method that Urban Meyer uses to create a team that has high effort throughout the season is to make them feel like they have a chip on the shoulder. Meyer told Scout.com that he likes it when his team is "angry".

"I want a pissed off football team," Meyer said. "I want a team that has a chip on their shoulders. Maybe something's been taken from you. Are you a team that's gonna get it?"

Before the 2006 National Championship game, Meyer was able to bring his Florida Gators to a peak by getting them angry and motivated.

According to a report in Bleacher Report and told in Meyer's book, there was about 10 feet worth of bulletin board material that was placed at the team hotel. "Half of it was real and half of it was made up. And the half that was made up, I signed 'Kirk Herbstreit of

ESPN'". (Herbstreit played college football at Ohio State, who were the opponent of the Gators in the championship game that year.)

"That made them angry, extremely angry. You tell a prideful group of men that have worked real hard that they don't belong somewhere. Any time you're dealing with people and say, 'By the way, you're not good enough to be here', especially if they've got a little pride, which that team had a lot of pride - yeah, we used that quite a bit."

It's important to note that angry does not mean out of control, or a team that wants to hurt the other team. As one player said, angry means "just having a chip on our shoulder. Coach Meyer talks about that all the time. You've got to play with a chip on your shoulder. You have to be angry, in a comfortable way though. You can't just go out there out of control angry."

Meyer views an angry team as a motivated team. "It's a coach's dream to coach an angry group of guys that are on a mission."

He also views an angry team as a hungry team, or a team that isn't satisfied with its current ranking.

"I love hungry teams. Complacent is a bad word. Satisfied is a bad word. Angry is a great word. Chip on your shoulder is what I want to see."

Attitude plays a big part in giving effort. Meyer wants to see all of his players come out to practice with high energy. If not, he sends the player back to the locker and tells them to come back out with more pep in their step.

"You can measure attitude," he says. "Be an energy-giver, don't be an energy-taker."

Break It Down to the Simplest Form

Throughout the many media reports on Meyer, it's very clear that he likes to create easy, simple reminders for his players. These short slogans are used to reinforce certain messages that Meyer would like his team to constantly remember.

These short, easy-to-remember terms are very useful for two reasons. One, it allows the players to know exactly what they have to do to be successful. For example, one of the first slogans he used with his players was to tell them to go "Plus 2". The thinking behind that saying was to encourage his players to go 2 steps past what was expected of them. So if the players were running sprints to the 10 yard line, then run for 2 steps more once after passing the finish line. Not only does this saying push his players to give their fullest effort on each play, but it also makes sure that each player finishes strong.

Another saying that Urban Meyer instilled into his team is "Four-to-six, A-to-B". According to Andy Staples of Sports Illustrated, Meyer taught this saying to his players because the average football play lasts between four to six seconds. "Meyer has preached about giving maximum effort for this brief stretch for years, but he never had it codified and prioritized like this," writes Staples.

These slogans allowed the players to easily remember what they needed to do in order to put in maximum effort.

Another reason why these short slogans are so useful is that a high level of thought is needed to craft them. Leading up to the National Championship game against Oregon, Meyer and his coaching staff studied Oregon's high-powered offense thoroughly. Through their extensive scouting, and carefully thinking about what they needed their players to do, they were able to create a gameplan to achieve victory. When sharing the strategy with their players, they broke it down to its simplest form.

16.

According to a report by Pete Thamel in Sports Illustrated, if Ohio State's defense could force Oregon to take longer than 16 seconds to snap the ball between each play, then they wouldn't be able to get in rhythm. Meyer wanted his players to simply focus on those 16 seconds. "Forget the Heisman winner at quarterback, the hype of the title game and the millions watching on TV," writes Thamel. "Eliminate 16, and you'll win."

To do that, Meyer and his staff placed the No. 16 all over the place. They put it up in the locker room. The put up signs of the No. 16 in the meeting rooms and at the team hotel. The strength coach of the team even ripped of the jersey off of the reserve defensive back who wore number 16, and forced him to wear a different number for the title game.

Thamel continues, "Part of Meyer's mad genius -- more than any X's or O's he moves on the grease board -- is his relentless ability to motivate. He emphasizes more themes than an English professor. He has more rallying cries than a rack of bumper stickers. There's pushing and pulling. There's prodding. Any motivational tactic will be exploited." He continues, "There are enough mottos, pictures and speeches to make a comatose frat guy rise up and run a 4.4."

As Ohio State's scout-team quarterback stated to Sports Illustrated, "If you have a problem being motivated here at Ohio State, there's actually something wrong with you."

Perhaps the most impactful motivational saying that Meyer had his championship winning team at Ohio State remember was given to him by a leadership consultant.

Tim Knight is a leadership consultant in Ohio who met Meyer at a fundraising party at the coach's home. After hearing what Knight did for his clients, Meyer immediately took advantage of this chance meeting and followed up by emailing Knight that evening and then inviting him to the football facility the next morning.

According to a report in the Wall Street Journal, Knight became a close partner to the Ohio State team during the 2014 season. Usually, outside leadership speakers or motivational coaches usually just drop in for a day and give a half-hour speech. However, Meyer had Knight work closely with his players and created a structure to develop leadership within his team.

The key formula that Meyer and Knight had all of the players remember is the following:

$$E + R = O$$

Event plus Responses equals Outcome.

Brian Knight, son of Tim, works with his father in teaching the formula to the Ohio State players. He explained the meaning of the formula to the website Eleven Warriors.

"$E + R = O$ represents the basic structure of how life works," Brian Knight told the website. "Events happen. You choose how to respond and an outcome is produce. The only thing you, I, or anyone has control over in that equation - in life - is how to respond. We call it "The R Factor," and it makes the difference between a good team and a championship team."

Brian Knight also mentions that it isn't play calls, or the right schemes that makes champions, which is a similar message that Meyer makes. Rather, your mindset and how you respond makes the difference.

"It's not bench press or 40 time or the right play call," Knight said. "It's how you respond when situations get difficult."

This mindset of being able to respond to an event and to create a favorable outcome was one of the key reasons why Ohio State was able to win the national championship. Despite having their top two quarterbacks go down with injuries, the team was able to rally behind third-string quarterback Cardale Jones.

There was no panic among the team. There was no victimization. There was no excuses. Cardale Jones stepped up and did his job. The team Responded to an Event (injuries of the two quarterbacks) and achieved an Outcome (national champs).

Review Questions:

1. What is the fuel that is driving your organization? You have a vision and a goal, but what are you doing to keep the desire for achieving that goal burning each day?

2. When was the last time you motivated your staff? Is the only time you think about motivation during the once-a-year annual retreat? Meyer thinks of ways to motivate his team every day. How often do you think about motivation?

3. Are you studying your situation so thoroughly that you can break down what you need to do in the simplest form? Meyer was able to come up with the No.16 because he took the time to study Oregon and knew exactly how to beat them. A simple "Try Hard" slogan is useless because it doesn't show your organization the exact way to victory. What simple messages are you giving your team to help them focus?

4. How do you respond to events? Do you feel sorry for yourself when events that weren't planned impact your organization? Are you letting events determine the outcome? Or are you responding to the events to determine the outcome?

5. How resilient is your organization? If a play breaks down, if a key employee leaves, will you be able to continue working at peak efficiency? Ohio State played in the Conference Championship Game, the National Semi-Final game, and the National Championship game with its 3rd string quarterback, and won them all. How would your organization perform if you lost your most important player?

Constant Learning

Leadership Must Be Taught

In order to have his coaches work effectively with their respective units, they must be able to lead the players, gain their trust, and be effective unit leaders. Like any large organization, these leaders are responsible for their own unit and must be able to properly manage the individuals.

In corporate America, millions of dollars is spent each year on leadership training and workshops. However, Meyer estimates that basically zero dollars is spent on developing the leadership abilities of coaches within the college system. The assumption is that football coaches are supposed to be natural leaders and know how to manage their players and be great leaders.

Meyer has taken the opposite track. He believes that everyone can learn to be a better leader, and has taken steps to incorporate leadership training into his program. During the offseason, his coaches went through a 5-week leadership training course that taught them how to be better unit leaders.

Meyer is fully committed to learning about leadership and having his staff grow as leaders. In fact, he believes so much in growing as a leader that if a person doesn't believe that they need leadership training, then that person probably won't be coaching at Ohio State for too long.

"If I ever see a guy who thinks that he's too good for a leadership workshop, then it's time to move on," Meyer said in a speech. "It's time to go somewhere else."

Learn from others

One of the things that Urban Meyer does constantly is learn from others. He is able to absorb information from all types of subjects and coaches, and is able to use it to his advantage.

According to an article published by the Wall Street Journal, Meyer's success has a lot to do with his ability to be a master imitator. "The one thing he does better than any coach is incorporate other ideas into his own," writes Ben Cohen.

Cohen gives an example of the spread offense, which is closely associated with Urban Meyer. However, the spread offense that Meyer uses was not created out of the blue by Meyer. Instead, "Meyer traveled the country as a young coach, picking off schemes from the pioneers, and tweaking the system for his own purposes," writes Cohen.

One of a common problem that successful coaches, executives, or managers face is that they become set in their ways once they hit a certain level of success. They believe that the strategies, methods, and structure that got them to the top are the only way to do things. People close to Meyer, however, believe that his "capacity to absorb information sets him apart from more stubborn coaches."

One example of Meyer adjusting his style involved the use of a huddle. During his championship runs at the University of Florida, Meyer was a big proponent of the huddle. With quarterback Tim Tebow, considered one of the best college football players ever and known for his strong leadership abilities, Meyer preferred to have his players use a huddle before each offensive play.

"In the old days, the stories of Joe Montana looking at Jerry Rice and winking at him, and there's still that intangible value of this great game of football: Let's you and me do this," Meyer stated. "It's harder when the guy you're winking at is 25 yards away" when the team runs a no-huddle offense.

However, the game of football has changed drastically in recent years. Speed and running an up-tempo system on offense has spread across both college football and the NFL. During his year off from coaching, Urban Meyer developed a friendship with Chip Kelly, who was then the head coach at Oregon and is now the coach of the Philadelphia Eagles.

When filling out his staff at Ohio State, Meyer hired Tom Herman as his offensive coordinator based on the recommendation from Kelly. Herman wanted to bring the same type of no-huddle approach to the Buckeyes.

Despite his reservations and personal preferences, Meyer adapted to the new environment and allowed Herman to run an up-tempo offense. "I didn't want to lose that huddle," Meyer said. "Obviously we've lost it." He realized that the no-huddle schemes were just the way that things were, and he had to adjust and accept it. "The stress that it puts on a defense, that's why we do it. You'd be crazy not to do it."

Review Questions:

1. Even after achieving success as a head coach and winning national championships, Urban Meyer still believes that he can learn from other coaches. He is fully aware that he can always improve as a coach and constantly searches out for new ideas. Do you still believe that you can learn? Do you believe that they way you do things is so successful that it is the only way to do things?

2. Are you adapting to the current environment in your industry? Are you holding on to certain beliefs, attitudes, and ways of doing things simply because "it's always been done this way"? Even if you have a preference for doing things a certain way, if the industry has changed, then you may be left behind if you don't adapt.

3. Are you allowing your staff to do their jobs? Do you think you can do their jobs better then them? Are you preventing them from incorporating changes because you personally don't want to? Are you letting a younger staff member who was trained in newer technology run free? Or are you attempting to control the innovation from your staff?

4. Are you reaching out to outside experts? Or do you think that you know everything that there is to know? Urban Meyer already won two national championships before he met Tim Knight, yet he had absolutely no hesitation in reaching out to him and having him talk to his players. Meyer didn't think that he was an expert in leadership, or that only the head coach could talk about leadership. Meyer didn't let his ego get in the way. He felt that another person could positively contribute to the development of his team, and let the other person come in and share his expertise.

5. If you are using outside consultants, are you integrating them into your program? As Tim Knight said, "There are a lot of quotes, posters, and best-selling authors that come in and talk to the team for a half-hour. But what Coach Meyer has done with us is brought a systematic, disciplined way of building these skills." If you are bringing in consultants or speakers, are you allowing them to fully integrate into your program? Or are you still trying to control their influence?

Part 2: Resources

Part 2 contains direct quotes and statement made by Urban Meyer, as well as quotes about Meyer made by other people. These statements provide a quick way of understanding the intensity, work ethic, and motivational techniques used by Meyer to achieve excellence.

Following the quotes, we list several books that Urban Meyer has publicly recommended. One of the book, Lone Survivor, was previously mentioned in the leadership section about creating a Clarity of Purpose. The other books have been mentioned by Meyer as playing a big impact in his own philosophy and mindset in creating champions.

Quotes, Statements, and Ideas from Urban Meyer

"If you start making excuses, players respond and use excuses. Excuses causes problems."

"If you don't have a chip on your shoulder, you'll lose like that," Meyer says while snapping his fingers twice.

"You can try to fix behavior, but it's unsustainable unless you fix the culture. I believe in that from the bottom of my gut."

"We don't have time to waste."

"Whether you're a broadcaster, whether you're a banker, whether you're a teacher, a coach, if you come out without passion and enthusiasm and focus, you're done."

"Be an energy giver, don't be an energy taker."

"When you're hit in the face - we all get hit in the face in work, family, or social situations or team situations - there are only two choices. You can be part of the problem, or you can be part of the solution."

"You can't function in today's era of college football without a superstar as a weight coach. That's more important than a coordinator or a line coach."

"Someone asked a question one time, 'When does the joy of winning disappear and the fear of losing or the agony of losing overtake that?' When that does, that's not good. That's not good for anyone. So I make sure that we enjoy the wins the best I can."

"The most important people are your players, and you can't grind them to the point where they're not enjoying the journey."

"When you're dealing with 18-21 year olds, you've got to give them something different than, 'Hey, play hard.'."

"It's so easy to be average."

"It takes a little something to be special, to be a great player."

"Did you push yourself to be great today? Did you do it? If you didn't, you lost a day, and we ain't got many days to lose."

"It takes time, effort, and guts to find out what the problem is."

"We're going to push your ass like it's never been pushed. Because what you got in you, we're going to find out. And if there's a touch of greatness in there, how cool would that be?"

"If I ever see a guy who thinks that he's too good for a leadership workshop, then it's time to move on. It's time to go somewhere else."

What People say about Urban Meyer

"His program is based on real. Everything about it is the truth. It's real, it's hard and kids thrive in it because it's developing them for something bigger than football. In this industry, there's too much fakeness and sales. When guys get a real coach, they'll do anything for him because that's what they really want."

"The way he does it is he gets to know them, he understands how to push each individual button, but he knows how to do it as a group, too. It's kind of old school, but he works on developing the total person. What does it take for you to be great? That's different for each of them, and he doesn't treat them all the same. He understands how to look at them individually and mold them from there. He's a master at it."

Zach Smith, Receivers Coach, Ohio State.

On adaptability and adjusting offense to meet the players strength:

"We did not try to fit a square peg in a round hole, and we still maintained our core beliefs of what we want to do offensively."

Tom Herman, Former Offensive Coordinator, Ohio State.

"We believe culture eats strategy for lunch. Strategy says 'This is the behavior I want.' Culture determines whether or not you get it."

Tim Knight, Leadership Consultant to Ohio State

"If there's something he can get from anyone else to help his team win, he's going to do that."

Former University of Texas Longhorns Head Coach Mack Brown

"He's the most astute listener I've ever met."

Ohio State Tight End Coach Tim Hinton

"He's done a tremendous, Emmy award-winning job coaching our coaches in philosophy, methodology and recruiting. I see it all. He's really into coaching."

"The cool part about him and being head coach is, he gets to get away. In February, he went away for a week. He'll read a book or two and he'll come back with something new. We call it enhancing. Rather than change what you do, you're enhances it. He's always trying to grow and get better."

Mickey Marotti, Ohio State Assistant Athletic Director for Football Sports Performance (Strength Coach)

"Coach Meyer is fanatical about teaching]."

"The guy is a wizard. In the past 18 months, I feel like I'm learning something every day, which is awesome, and I'm 10 times the coach I was before I got here."

Tom Herman, Former Ohio State Offensive Coordinator and current University of Houston Head Coach.

"He never stops trying to figure out another way to motivate players, improve the program, get coaches to coach better. That's the secret recipe to him. It's not scheme. The scheme is fine, but there's too much emphasis on that. Get your guys to play fast and get them motivated, that's your value as a coach."

Steve Addazio, Head Coach, Boston College

Books recommended by Urban Meyer

LEAD---For God's Sake!, by Todd G. Gongwer

One of the books that Urban Meyer has said that changed his life is called LEAD...For God's Sake. The book uses the examples of very successful individuals and their quest for excellence, and how that quest can lead them to some difficult places.

Meyer was given the book by ESPN College Football Analyst Todd Blackledge after Meyer joined the network after resigning from the University of Florida. He started reading the book while on a visit to Stanford as part of his duties at ESPN. While exercising and reading the book, Meyer states that he couldn't flip the pages fast enough.

According to an article in ESPN, Meyer "ran with the book in his hand, stopping on campus to sit and read. He ran an hour, read an hour, back and forth. The sun climbed, and he couldn't turn the pages fast enough. He finished that day and emailed the author from his phone, saying, "This is the most profound book I've ever read."

Lone Survivor, by Marcus Luttrell

This book is about a Navy Seal who went behind enemy lines in Afghanistan in order to document the activities of an Al Qaeda leader. Of the four Navy Seals that went on the mission, only one survived.

Marcus Luttrell writes about how he survived the ordeal, and writes about how he became a Navy Seal. Meyer has stated that he learned a lot about the training, culture, and dedication that comes from being a part of an elite unit.

Urban Meyer originally read the book while he was still coaching at the University of Florida, and has raved about the book every since.

"I'm reading 'Lone Survivor', a great book out now. I'm three-quarters of the way through it. There are so many great lessons. The ultimate motivation, the ultimate unselfish approach, is the men and women who are serving overseas. Why not learn from them?", Meyer told the media back in 2009. "What's our mojo going to be this year? It's going to be lessons I've learned from this book. There are so many great lessons to be learned."

After winning the national championship, Urban Meyer was still talking about the impact that the book had on him. At a coaches clinic in April 2015, Meyer told the attendees that the book still gives him motivation.

"On page 15 of Lone Survivor, the book, right on the top. I've read that son of a gun hundreds of times. Whenever I want to re-motivate myself and re-organize myself for spring practice, for offseason, I'll do it again this summer, I turn to page 15 and here's what an elite soldiers says. 'The clarity of purpose is inspirational'. That's all it says", the website Eleven Warriors quoted him as saying.

Change or Die, by Alan Deutschman

Another book that Urban Meyer publicly recommends to people is the book Change or Die. An article in ESPN talked about the book after Meyer burned himself out at Florida.

"For instance, there's a book he loves, written for business executives, called 'Change or Die,' which shaped his ideas about altering the behavior of athletes. He has talked about the book in speeches, invited the author to Gainesville, handed out copies, and never, not once, did he realize the book almost perfectly described him."

On the author's website, Meyer wrote a little blurb recommending the book.

"I was really intrigued by the book Change or Die. There are some very powerful concepts and ideas that strike at the psychological core of getting people to change. Most people are looking for a quick fix when it comes to the culture of change in an organization, but Alan makes it clear that this is not an easy process. This book is an invaluable resource for anyone who is in a management or leadership position."

Additional information and links to the books are available at leadershipcasestudies.com.

Key Takeaways

1. Every rep matter, and there is a winner and loser for each rep.

2. Address the issues in front of you directly.

3. Have the hard, honest conversations with people when needed.

4. In order for people to work hard for you, they need to trust you.

5. You get people to trust you by showing them you are a person of character, that you are competent, and by connecting with them by caring about their well-being.

6. Leadership can be learned, and you must put in the effort to learn it.

7. No matter how successful you are, you can still learn from other people.

8. Be adaptable. Situations and the environment change everyday, so the way you achieved success yesterday may not work today.

9. Events may be outside of your control, but how you respond to the events will determine the outcome.

10. Create a clarity of purpose to inspire you everyday.

Additional Leadership Case Studies

The Management Ideas of Nick Saban

The Turnaround Strategies of Jim Harbaugh

The Strategy Concepts of Bill Belichick

The Work Ethic of Tom Brady, Peyton Manning, and Aaron Rodgers

The Leadership Lessons of Gregg Popovich

The Team Building Strategies of Steve Kerr

About Leadership Case Studies

Leadership Case Studies provides brief reports and analysis on successful individuals. We focus on the habits, strategies, and mindsets of high-performing people in the sports, business, and entertainment industries.

Links to the case studies articles, videos and speeches are all listed on the website.

Started in July 2015, Leadership Case Studies released its first case study on University of Alabama Football Coach Nick Saban, winner of 4 national championships.

Website:
http://www.leadershipcasestudies.com

Made in the USA
Las Vegas, NV
24 January 2021